W9-BXB-318

GO FOR IT!™

TRACK & FIELD

FOR BOYS AND GIRLS

START RIGHT AND COMPETE WELL

by Bill Gutman

with Illustrations
by Ben Brown

MARSHALL CAVENDISH
CORPORATION

GREY CASTLE PRESS

Marshall Cavendish Edition, Freeport, New York.

No part of this publication may be reproduced in whole or in part, or stored
in a retrieval system, or transmitted in any form or by any means, electronic,
mechanical, photocopying, recording, or otherwise, without written permission
of Grey Castle Press.

Published by arrangement with Grey Castle Press, Lakeville, Ct.

Printed in the USA

The Library of Congress Cataloging in Publication Data

Gutman, Bill.
    Track & Field : start right and play well / by Bill Gutman ; with
illustrations by Ben Brown.
        p.   cm. — (Go for it!)
    ''Published by arrangement with Grey Castle Press, Lakeville, Ct.''—
T.p. verso.
    Summary: Describes the history and competitions in track and field
and provides instruction in the techniques of the various events.
    ISBN 0-942545-87-7 (lib. bdg.)
    1. Track-athletics—Juvenile literature. [1. Track and field.]
I. Brown, Ben, 1921–   Ill. II. Title. III. Title: Track and
field. IV. Series: Gutman, Bill. Go for it!
GV1060.5.G88   1990
796.42—dc20   89-7378
                                                                          CIP
                                                                           AC

Photo credits: Focus On Sports, page 8; UPI/Bettmann, page 7.

Special thanks to: Terry Horton, varsity track coach, Arlington High School,
LaGrangeville, N.Y.

Picture research: Omni Photo Communications, Inc.

ABOUT THE AUTHOR

Bill Gutman is the author of over 70 books for children and young adults. The majority of his titles have dealt with sports, in both fiction and non-fiction, including "how-to" books. His name is well-known to librarians who make it their business to be informed about books of special interest to boys and reluctant readers. He lives in Poughquag, New York.

ABOUT THE ILLUSTRATOR

Ben Brown's experience ranges from cartoonist to gallery painter. He is a graduate of the High School of Music & Art in New York City and the University of Iowa Art School. He has been a member of the National Academy of Design and the Art Students' League. He has illustrated government training manuals for the disadvantaged (using sports as themes), and his animation work for the American Bible Society won two blue ribbons from the American Film Festival. He lives in Great Barrington, Massachusetts.

In order to keep the instructions in this book as simple as possible, the author has chosen in most cases to use "he" to signify both boys and girls.

A BRIEF HISTORY

Men have been running and jumping since the beginning of time, making it very difficult to say just when track and field competition began. Whatever the country or the language, one person has probably said to another, "Bet I can run faster than you."

It is known, however, that athletic contests involving running were held as part of religious festivals in the days of ancient Greece. In 776 B.C., the first Olympic Games took place at Olympia on the eastern coast of the Peloponnesian peninsula. Besides athletic contests, there were contests in music, oral debate and theater.

Then, as now, the games were held every four years, and the tradition continued for several centuries. There weren't too many sporting events until the warlike Spartans became involved during the eighteenth Olympics. They began a pentathlon-like competition that had running, jumping, javelin and discus throwing.

After that, sports became a bigger and bigger part of these ancient games. There was more running and jumping, as well as other contests, such as boxing and wrestling. When the Romans continued the Olympic tradition, even chariot races became part of the agenda. But finally, in 394 A.D., the Roman emperor Theodosius called a halt to the Games. He felt they were more pagan than Christian. Religion still played a large role in these early track and athletic contests.

With the death of the ancient Olympics, the early days of track and field died as well. The sport really didn't come back on an organized level until the nineteenth century in England. At that time, many public school and university students began competing with each other in track events.

In 1849, the Royal Military Academy held the first real track and field meet of modern times. Finally, in the 1860s, the sport began to grow. By 1866, the first English Championships were put on by the newly formed Amateur Athletic Club. The athletes were not paid to compete. For the most part, track and field has remained an amateur sport, though the rules have changed in the 1980s.

In 1880, the Amateur Athletic Association was formed in England and has conducted the national championships there ever since. By that time, the sport had also spread to the United States. The New York Athletic Club had been formed in 1868 and was primarily a track and field club. Then, in 1887, the Amateur Athletic Union (AAU) of the United States began. It started as an association of track and field clubs and has governed the sport in America ever since.

By this time, the sport was becoming established in many countries. And in 1896, the Olympic Games were started once again. This time they were purely for international athletic competition.

The Olympics grew to become the pinnacle of track and field. With the games being held every four years, the great track stars soon began to compete. Perhaps the most well-known early star of track and field was Jim Thorpe, an American Indian better known for his football skills. At the 1912 Olympics, he won both the pentathlon and decathlon. He was hailed as the world's greatest athlete and then returned to play football for many more years.

In the 1920s, the track world was thrilled by the feats of a runner named Paavo Nurmi, the "Flying Finn" from Finland. Besides breaking many records, he participated in three Olympic Games: in 1920, 1924 and 1928. He ran in 10 races and won seven

6

Jesse Owens was one of the greatest track and field competitors of all time. He won four gold medals in the 1936 Olympics in Berlin, Germany.

Jackie Joyner-Kersee is a record-setting star who won two gold medals in the 1988 Olympics.

of them. The other three times he was second. Nurmi also set world records at 12 different distances, from one mile to 20,000 meters. Nurmi, and others like him, made the sport of track and field more popular than ever.

By 1932, track was getting even bigger in the United States. Women had been allowed to compete in the Olympics for the first time in 1928—but only in a few events. In 1932, they were back. One of the stars was an American woman named Babe Didrikson. She set world records in the javelin and 80 meter hurdles to win a pair of gold medals. She later became a champion golfer, known then as Babe Didrikson Zaharias, and is remembered today as one of the greatest female athletes of all time.

In 1936, a black American track star became a world hero. His name was Jesse Owens, and he won four gold medals in the Olympics, which were held in Berlin, Germany. Germany was then under the leadership of the world's most destructive dictator, Adolph Hitler. Among other things, Hitler's Nazi regime said that blacks were inferior. Because of this, Jesse Owens was under a great deal of pressure competing in Germany. But he won gold medals in the 100 and 200 meter dashes, the long jump and the 400 meter relay. Needless to say, Hitler did not like that.

To many, track and field is the showcase of the Olympic Games. But many records have been broken, apart from the Olympics. In 1954, a British runner named Roger Bannister did something many people thought impossible. For the first time in history, he ran the mile in less than four minutes (3:59.4). Today, the sub-four-minute mile is very common, showing how track records have moved forward in modern times.

The Olympic Games remain a world showcase, even though they have often been hurt by politics. Different nations, including the United States, have at one time or another refused to participate in the Games. Many fine athletes have lost a chance at a gold medal because of this.

Yet the great track stars have become as well known as famous athletes in other sports. Bob Mathias and Rafer Johnson were both Olympic decathlon winners who later made motion pictures. Mathias was also elected to Congress. Olympic sprint champion Bob Hayes became a star receiver for the Dallas Cowboys in the National Football League. Sprinter Wilma Rudolph became a national heroine after three gold medals in the 1960 Games. Hurdler Edwin Moses has become a world famous celebrity by being the best in the world in his event for well over a decade.

Even in the 1988 Olympics, track and field stars made the news. Sprinter and long jumper Carl Lewis was a standout performer, as were women stars Florence Griffith-Joyner and Jackie Joyner-Kersee. Like all the champions before them, they reached the top through hard work and dedication.

Track and field is a sport for everyone, boy and girl, man and woman, young and old. You're never too young to start nor too old to continue. It's a sport that keeps people trim and fit, and it's well worth learning.

ORGANIZATION

While running races may be the oldest sport in the world, organized track and field has changed greatly in the decade of the 1980s. The sport is still controlled by the International Amateur Athletic Federation (IAAF) throughout the world. In the United States, the Amateur Athletic Union (AAU) still rules. However, the times have forced both bodies to change.

Track and field has always been an amateur sport. That means that the athletes do not get paid. There has never been prize money given for an Olympic victory. In America and Europe, it has been traditional for track and field athletes to pay their own way. They often had to work while training in their free time.

But when the Soviet Union and the other Communist countries of Eastern Europe began competing at the international level, things began to change. In those countries, the state pays for its athletes to live while they train. That has made it much easier for Soviet and Eastern European athletes to prepare for competition.

Gradually, the people who controlled track in America realized that more had to be done for their athletes. Today, top athletes are not paid directly for winning amateur meets. But they can still make a great deal of money by participating in the sport. They have sponsors, have all their travel and expense money paid and do compete in some meets where there is prize money. In addition, they can endorse products and have other business interests connected to the sport. This enables them to be full-time athletes, which is necessary today in order to compete.

Track has changed in other ways, too. For years, the sport was dominated by men. Even though women began competing in the Olympics in 1928, it took years for them to be thought of as equal with men. It took even longer at the school level.

Right into the 1970s, many high schools just didn't have track programs for girls. Finally, in 1976, the government passed new laws that forced schools to offer women's sports programs equal to men's. Track has greatly benefited from these new laws.

Now, both boys and girls participate in track by the thousands. For example, the Colgate Women's Games in 1980 had more than 20,000 entrants, including girls as young as six and older women who hoped to make the Olympics. Road races and mini-marathons are now common with young and old, male and female, competing on an equal basis. There is some kind of track program at most elementary schools, and almost all high schools compete against each other. The sport has tens of thousands of participants throughout the country and many more throughout the world.

LEARNING ABOUT TRACK AND FIELD

Getting Ready To Compete

Anyone who likes to run and jump can compete in track and field. Track includes all running and hurdling events, both sprints and distance running. Field events include the high jump and long jump. They also include pole vaulting, the shot put, discus and javelin throws. However, because young people just starting out do not usually compete in those last four events, they will not be discussed in this book.

Track is both an individual and a team sport. A runner or jumper is always trying to improve time or distance. In practice, it's easy for someone to see if he or she is getting better. While runners are competing against the clock, they are also competing against other runners. Sometimes a runner will win a race without beating his best time. That's all right, too. In longer races,

The stopwatch is a valuable tool for all runners. By using it, both sprinters and distance runners can follow their improvement, down to a hundredth of a second.

strategy is very important. Sometimes it's better to run a smart race than a fast one.

However, it is not enough to simply enjoy running or jumping. To compete in track, a young person must be both mentally and physically tough. No one can become a top track star without a great deal of very hard work. Regular training is a must. A person competing in track must take care of his body at all times. Boys and girls must learn to watch what they eat and work out every day. Muscles must be kept toned and stretched.

Competitors must also have a regular training schedule. The best way is to have a coach set it up. He will know how to prepare for the different events. For example, a sprinter will train differently from a distance runner. A high jumper will have a different workout than a long jumper. Hurdlers must do special exercises to get ready for that event.

Like other athletes, runners will sometimes have to work through pain. Otherwise, they will have to run at slightly less than their best. At these times, it takes a great deal of will power to still perform and work hard. Even when a runner is in top shape, mental toughness is often the deciding factor.

For example, if a runner is racing someone of about the same ability, the winner will often be the one who wants victory more. This means the person who is willing to push just a little harder, drive himself to run faster than the person alongside him. Desire has always played a big role in track and field. All the great ones have had a special will to win.

Some runners like to set long-term goals. This may mean working toward a certain time or distance in an event. It may also mean winning a certain race, or becoming a champion. Or it may even be making the Olympic team. Setting long-term goals gives the athlete something to work for over a period of time. It keeps him or her going.

Short-term goals are often set by the coach. They can simply be to achieve a personal best by a certain date. Then to top that standard again the next time out. Or it may be to become the best in an event within the team, or to defeat a certain rival for the first time. The short-term goal is something that is always right ahead. When the athlete reaches it, he knows he is making progress and is just a step closer to that long-range goal.

To become a better runner or jumper, a young person should really be part of an organized team. Some runners enjoy working and training on their own. But for someone just starting in the sport, having a coach is important because the coach is in the best position to watch each member of the team and decide which event is best for that person.

Running events from 60 yards to 200 yards are the sprint events. The 440 yard (quarter mile) and the 880 yard (half mile) runs are middle distances. The mile and two mile runs are thought of as distance events. This is true for young runners right into high school. Then, even the 440 becomes a sprint. Olympic runners now go all out over the 400 meter distance.

One word about yards versus meters. In the United States, distances have always been measured in yards. The rest of the world usually measures distance in meters.

A meter is a few inches longer than a yard. In the Olympics, for

1 YARD
36 INCHES

1 METER
39.37 INCHES

A meter is about three and a third inches longer than a yard. Since distances are measured in meters in most parts of the world, it is a good idea for young track athletes to know the difference.

example, runners compete in events of 100 meters, 200, 400 and 800 meters. Instead of a mile, they run 1,500 meters. Today, meters are being used more and more in the United States. From this point on, the different races will be referred to mostly in meters.

To be a sprinter, a runner must be very quick. He must also have good reflexes for quick starts. In addition, strength is needed, since the sprinter must get up to full speed quickly and drive down the track without letting up.

A middle-distance runner must also have good speed, but he needs stamina as well. Stamina is the ability to run hard without getting tired. All runners get tired, but those with the most stamina can go harder and longer. As a runner gets to the longer distances, speed becomes less important. Sometimes two runners who are close must sprint for the finish at the end of a long race. It isn't always the faster runner who wins; it is the one with the most endurance.

Long jumpers must also have great speed. The more speed a long jumper can achieve as he sprints down the runway, the better momentum he will have going into his jump. He must also have strong legs to get him off the board and into the air.

High jumpers must have good "spring" in their legs. They must naturally be able to leap high. It may also help to be tall, but this is not necessary to all good high jumpers. It is more important for a high jumper to have the proper form and to know how to get the most out of the event.

There is one event that hasn't been mentioned—the hurdles. This event combines speed with jumping ability, as well as form and timing. The coach will probably pick people he feels can develop this skill, and he will make them into hurdlers.

Like other sports, track and field can be fun. But it is also hard work. Anyone who wants just the fun and not the hard work should not join a track team. He should just run on his own. It is still a very good and healthy thing to do.

Equipment

Anyone who has ever watched a track meet knows that competitors do not need a great deal of equipment. Runners wear only shorts and jerseys. They may also have a warm-up suit and maybe a sweat suit for cool days. However, there is one piece of equipment that is very important for every runner: shoes.

A serious runner cannot train and compete in only a pair of sneakers. Sneakers are fine for running around the house or playing a pick-up game of football, baseball or basketball. To train and compete in track, a special pair of shoes are recommended.

There are three basic kinds of shoes for track—training flats, racing flats and spikes. Training flats are worn most of the time in practice. A good training flat will cushion the foot while giving it support and stability. A racing flat does the same thing, but it is lighter in weight because it is made for speed. Spikes are like racing flats and are worn on certain kinds of tracks by sprinters and hurdlers.

It may be even more important for young runners to have the right kind of shoes. Because they are still growing, they must protect feet, ankles, legs and knees from excessive shock. Continuous running with the wrong kind of shoes can lead to serious problems with feet and legs, especially in the joints.

The way to avoid this is by wearing a well-cushioned shoe.

Every runner must have a well-fitting pair of training shoes (flats). The coach can tell each competitor which type of shoe is suitable for his or her event. On certain kinds of tracks, the sprinters will wear shoes with replaceable spikes on the soles only.

Runners' feet and legs take a tremendous pounding. Cushioning helps absorb the pounding. When a runner is trying on shoes, he should bounce up and down and maybe even take a few running steps. The shoes should feel springy, but not spongy or mushy. Shoes that are too soft are not good, either.

Running shoes should also be flexible. They should bend easily with the runner's foot inside. A stiff shoe will cause too much stress on the foot. There should also be a stiff insert in the heel of the shoe. This is called the *counter* and serves to hold the heel in place. Then the shoes won't wobble from side to side when they're in use.

Sprinters and hurdlers wear shoes with sharp spikes that look like nails. There are about six or seven of these spikes in an oval shape around the edge of the sole. With the better shoes, the spikes unscrew. That way, they can be changed if they break or wear out. Only some surfaces require spikes. The length of the spikes depends on the kind of track, another reason they are changeable.

The coach will tell his runners the best type of shoe to buy. He'll know the type of tracks the team will be using during the season and what kind of shoe is best for everyone on the team. If a runner is serious about track, he should always buy the best pair of shoes he can. That's how important running shoes are.

Two words of warning. Ultralight shoes do not have as much cushioning as heavier shoes. If a runner wants to wear this kind of lightweight shoe in a race, that's fine. But he should always go back to the heavier training shoe for his workouts. Wearing the light shoes too often could hurt his feet.

Also, runners must be careful about wearing shoes for too long. A pair of worn-out shoes cannot give the foot the proper support. If a runner waits too long to get new shoes, he may not have enough time to break them in. For that reason, runners should get their new shoes when there is still some life in the old ones.

That way, they can begin breaking the new shoes in slowly while still using the old ones.

Learning How To Warm Up

Knowing how to warm up before practice or a race is very important for all track and field performers. A runner who does not warm up or stretch constantly can easily pull a muscle, and a pulled muscle can keep a runner out of action for a long time.

Today, we know much more about muscles and the body than we did years ago. All coaches will be able to give their teams a list of warm-up exercises. The muscles must be fully stretched and loose before doing any hard training or running. The only time the warm up is not quite as important is when the workout is light, with perhaps just some easy running or jogging.

Warm-up exercises should be done slowly. When a muscle is being stretched, it should be held in the stretched position for several seconds. Don't just stretch and release quickly. Before doing warm-up exercises, runners should get their bodies ready by jogging slowly around the track once or twice, and maybe doing a few jumping jacks. That way, they won't be stretching stone-cold muscles.

From there, the runner can do some very basic exercises, such as push-ups and sit-ups. The exercises should be done slowly and smoothly. There is no need to do them to exhaustion. Now it's time to begin some light stretching.

Toe touching is a good way to start. The feet should be kept close together and the legs straight. Then the runner should bend from the waist until he is touching his toes with his fingertips. This position should be held for a few seconds. Once the muscles are loose and stretched, he can touch his fingers to the ground, then his palms. The lower he goes, the more the leg muscles will stretch.

The *split stretch* is a similar exercise. It is done with the feet

The proper warm-up is a very important part of track and field. A runner, hurdler or jumper who doesn't warm up can easily pull a muscle. The warm-up can begin with some simple toe touches and side stretching to begin loosening up the muscles. Another good warm-up exercise is the split stretch, shown above. With feet spread apart and legs straight, bend at the waist, touching the left hand to the right toe. Then straighten up and touch the right hand to the left toe. All stretching exercises should be done slowly, and held for five to ten seconds in the stretched position.

spread wide apart, the legs held straight. Bending at the waist, the runner touches the right hand to the left toe, then the left hand to the right toe. In between each touch, the runner should stand straight up.

Side stretches are another good exercise to do at the beginning. Simply put one hand on the hip and hold the other over the head with the arm bent at the elbow. Then lean to the side with the hand on the hip. Hold the position before reversing the hands and leaning to the other side. This exercise will help to loosen arm, shoulder and rib cage muscles.

Now it's time to really loosen the muscles. One exercise that nearly every runner does is the *hamstring stretch*. The hamstrings are located in the back of the thigh, and a pulled hamstring muscle is not an unusual injury for runners. To stretch the ham-

20

The hamstring stretch is a perfect warm up for the tendons behind the thighbone and knee. Extend one leg on a support, such as a railing or bench, keeping it straight at the knee. Then, bending the other knee slightly, lean forward at the waist, sliding the hands up toward the ankle. The hamstring muscles behind the leg will stretch out. Hold it for about 10 seconds, unless there is pain or discomfort. Then change legs and do it again. To really loosen the muscles well, each leg can be stretched five times.

strings, a person finds a bar or bench about waist high. He then places one leg on the support, keeping it straight. Bending the other leg at the knee just slightly, he leans forward slowly over the leg that is on the support.

As the runner slides his hands down his leg toward his foot, he will feel the hamstring muscle stretch. After holding the position for perhaps 10 seconds, he should straighten up slowly. Then he should reverse his legs and repeat the exercise. This should be done perhaps five times with each leg, but it should not be done to the point of pain or discomfort. The more the exercise is done, the looser the muscle should become. Then it should be easier to bend over further and slide the hands right down over the foot.

Another good leg exercise is the *hurdler's stretch*. This is done by sitting down with the legs spread wide apart. One leg is then folded back and tucked tight to the buttocks. Then the runner rocks forward from the waist while stretching the hands toward the outstretched leg.

The position should be held a few seconds, then the legs reversed. The stretch should be done five times on each side, again without causing pain. It will work on the muscles in the back of the leg and in the lower back. Even though it's called the hurdler's stretch, it should be done by everyone on the team.

Another exercise done from a sitting position is the *groin stretch*. The knees should be apart and the soles of the feet together. Grabbing the soles of the feet with the hands, the runner then pulls his feet back toward the groin while leaning forward slowly. The runner should keep leaning until his forehead touches his feet or he begins to feel pain. When he has leaned as far as he can, the runner should hold the position for about 10 seconds. This exercise should also be done five times.

This is the basic position from which to begin the hurdler's stretch. The exercise not only loosens muscles in the back of the legs, but also in the lower back. It should be done by all track athletes. To begin, sit on the ground with legs spread apart, then double one leg to the rear with the foot pointed outwards.

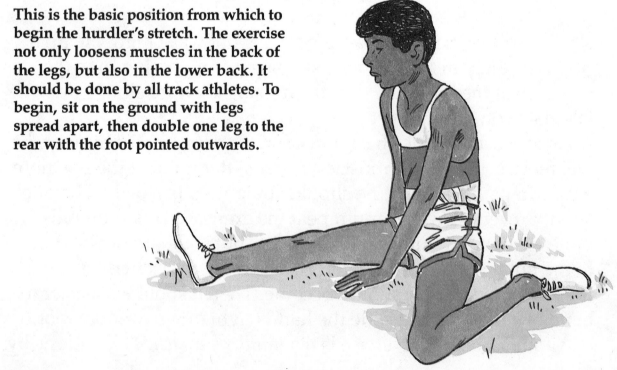

There are two exercises that can be done while lying on the back. The first is called the *back roll*. With the hands outstretched on the ground, the runner should bring his legs straight up, knees straight, then over his head until his feet touch the ground behind him. After about 10 seconds, the legs should be eased down, then raised again. This is good for hips and back.

The final exercise is another *back stretch*. With this one, one leg is raised at a time, knee bent, and then pulled toward the stomach with both hands. When the leg has been pulled as far as it will go without pain, the position is held for about 10 seconds. The leg should then be released and the opposite one raised. Each leg should be pulled five times.

This basic warm-up routine will get the runner ready for a workout or race. Different coaches may want to add other exercises or give their runners their own routines. All warm-up exercises are similar and do the job of stretching the muscles.

Next rock forward from the waist, moving the hands toward the outstretched foot. The further you lean, the more the muscles will be stretched. Hold the position for five or ten seconds, but not if there is any pain. Then reverse the legs and do it again. The exercise can be repeated several times with each leg.

Another very good exercise for the all-important leg and back muscles is the back roll. It's begun by lying flat on the back, then raising the legs keeping the knees straight. The legs should be brought all the way over the head and then down behind the head until the toes touch the ground. The final position should be held for five seconds. Then the legs can be eased down before the exercise is repeated.

A variation of the back roll is the back stretch. Once again the runner lies on his back. This time only one leg is raised with the knee bent. The leg should be grasped behind the thigh with the knee bent. The leg should be grasped behind the thigh with both hands and pulled tight toward the belly. The position should be held for five to ten seconds. Then the leg is released and the other leg raised and pulled tight. Each leg should be stretched five times.

When a runner finishes his training or race, he should not just sit down and stop. Cooling down is important so the muscles don't tighten. This cooling down can simply consist of some jogging and bending. Some runners prefer to also do some of their stretching exercises after their workout as well.

Learning To Be A Sprinter

Sprinting is a very simple thing. It just calls for a runner to go as hard as he can for the entire length of the race. The sprints are relatively short races because no runner can go that hard over a long distance.

The primary ingredient in sprinting is speed. A slow runner simply cannot be a sprinter, but a fast runner can get faster by knowing how to start and how to run hard right to the tape. It is the speed of the arms and legs that tells how fast a runner might be. The more steps a runner can take per second, the faster he will run.

It has been said that to become a good sprinter, a runner must be able to take at least four and a half steps per second. This is called ''natural muscle speed'' and it is the starting point for every sprinter. If a runner does not have enough muscle speed, he should think more about middle or long distance running.

Once a coach begins to work with a good, natural sprinter, the sprinter will start to improve his technique. Believe it or not, many fast runners do not really know how to sprint. Their running styles contain many extra, wasted movements, slowing them down. In a short sprint, every tenth of a second is important.

The coach will work at eliminating these wasted movements. Once they're gone, the coach will then concentrate on making the right movements stronger and smoother. For the sprinter, the right movements begin by running on the balls of his feet. This is

Sprint action features high knee action and a hard, rhythmic pumping of the arms. The runner should take long strides, and stay on the balls of his or her feet for the entire race.

a must and is also the reason why sprinters' shoes have spikes only on the soles, not the heels.

A sprinter's stride should not be too long or too short. An overly long stride will tire the runner quickly. The short, choppy stride just won't cover the ground quickly enough. Each sprinter must find a natural stride that feels comfortable. The coach can tell if it's too short or too long.

Sprinters also use a high knee drive when they run. For example, as the knee is brought up, the thigh should be just about level with the track. The hands can be cupped, but they should be relaxed. If a runner closes his fists tightly, he will cause too much tension in the arms.

Pumping the arms is also important, since the arms help drive the body forward. A good, steady arm pump will find the hands moving from the hip to the shoulder and back again. A sprinter should also avoid any extra head movement. The head should be held steady, eyes looking straight ahead. The sprinter should concentrate on one thing—the end of the race. He must break the tape in the fastest possible time.

Perhaps the most important part of the race for a sprinter is the start. A quick start will enable a runner to beat another runner with the same speed, or even one a little faster. This is especially true in the shorter races. The start is something a runner should practice again and again.

Years ago, runners would scuff out shallow holes in the track with their spikes. They would then place the soles of their feet in the holes and push off that way. Today, sprinters have starting blocks to help them get a fast start.

Starting blocks have a pair of adjustable foot supports that are slightly curved to fit the contour of the foot. They are mounted on

Used by all sprinters, the starting blocks are very important pieces of track equipment. Both styles of blocks shown here are adjustable so that each runner will feel comfortable with his or her foot placement. The blocks anchor to the track, allowing the runner to push off hard at the start of the race.

a metal shaft that has a spike on both ends so the blocks can be driven into the ground right behind the starting line.

The front end of the shaft should be about 9 or 10 inches behind the starting line. The foot supports should be anywhere from 12 to 18 inches behind the line. Because runners start differently, the rear support can be as close as two inches to the front support or as far as 14 or 16 inches from it.

As a rule of thumb, the runner's strongest leg is in the rear position at the start. The strongest leg is the one used to kick a football. The rear leg will then take the first full stride.

Some sprinters prefer to keep their feet close together in the blocks. Others tend to spread them far apart. Generally, a young runner should begin by placing the rear foot about six inches or so behind the front heel. The blocks are adjusted accordingly. Unless a runner feels very uncomfortable starting this way, he should try it for a while before changing the settings. If he feels a change is in order, then he should speak with his coach.

Next comes the actual starting sequence. The starter begins by telling the runners to ''Take your marks!'' At this command, the sprinter, who is already fully warmed up and standing with his toes on the starting line, will bend down and place his feet into the blocks. He will do this one foot at a time, making sure his toes are touching the track.

Still relaxed and breathing steadily, the runner will place the knee of his rear foot on the track alongside his front foot. He will then place his hands a shoulder's width apart on the track just behind the starting line. The thumb faces inward and the fingers outward, forming a support for his weight. The eyes should be focused downward or on a spot a few feet in front of the line.

The second command is, ''Get set!'' When he hears this, the sprinter will raise his hips to the height of his shoulders. He will also shift his weight forward to his hands. The knee of his front

The sprinter begins by standing with his toes on the starting line. At the command, "Take your marks," he will bend down and place both his hands on the track, just behind the starting line. Next he will place both feet firmly against the blocks, the rear foot always being placed first. When his feet are in place, his hands are brought back just behind the starting line, the thumb and fingers of each hand forming a bridge to support the runner's weight. The runner now awaits the next command with the knee of his rear leg still on the ground.

At the command, "Get set," the runner lifts his knee off the track, then raises his hips until they are almost level with his shoulder. He will lean forward so that his shoulders are almost even with the starting line and his weight is being supported by both his hands and feet. He should then raise his head and look at a spot 8 or 10 yards down the track.

The gun usually sounds within several seconds of the "get set" command. The sprinter must be ready to explode out of the blocks with a great deal of power. He will push hard against the block with his front leg, while at the same time bringing his rear leg forward to propel his body into motion. At the same time, he begins the hard pumping motion with his arms that will help him get up to full speed quickly.

foot should be bent at about a 90 degree angle at this point. The eyes should then be focused 8 to 10 yards down the track.

Now it's time to wait for the starter's gun. The perfect start means breaking from the blocks at the sound of the gun. If a runner jumps the gun, or moves before it sounds, it's a false start, and all the runners must come back. Either one or two false starts disqualify a runner, depending on the level of the competition.

There are usually two or three seconds between "Get set" and the gun. At the sound, the rear leg pushes out of the blocks, while the arm on the opposite side pumps hard forward. The front leg also drives hard against the block. Both legs must push forward, not up. The angle of the body will be low to the ground for the first 10 to 15 yards. The first strides will also be shorter as the sprinter pumps hard with both arms and legs to reach full speed as fast as he can.

Once out of the blocks, the sprinter must propel him-self forward. During the first 15 or 20 yards, he will continue to lean forward and pump his arms hard, gradually beginning to straighten his body into the normal running position.

Gradually the sprinter's body will straighten, and his stride will extend as he continues to pump his arms. It takes good reflexes, quickness and a great deal of strength to burst out of the blocks. And it should be a burst. Many a fast runner has been left behind in the blocks. That can mean starting the race five or six yards behind before reaching full stride.

Once the runner is out of the blocks and up to full speed, he simply has to run the race. However, there are still certain things he must remember. In the short sprints, an indoor 50 or outdoor 100 meter, for example, the start is even more important. The trick after reaching full speed is staying there.

Running at top speed, the leg muscles tire very quickly. In a very short race like the 50, it's a matter of a good start and reaching full speed just about when the race ends. No problem there. But in the 100, it's a bit different. A runner might take nearly half the race to reach full speed. Then he can run maybe 25 yards at

For the remainder of the race, the sprinter should concentrate on being smooth and relaxed. He must maintain high knee action and pump his arms in a steady rhythm. Sprinters may clench their fists loosely. A tightly clenched fist would put too much tension on the arms. The trick is to maintain speed and not slow down late in the race. Though a runner may lunge at the tape, he should concentrate on running to a point 5 to 15 yards beyond the finish line.

top speed before his muscles start to tire. The trick for the last yards of the race is not to slow down.

Sprinters must run relaxed. They have to go from their starting burst to their running stride without slowing down. It's a mistake for a sprinter to try to go even faster in the middle of the race. It really can't be done. Instead, the runner must stay smooth and relaxed.

When a sprinter seems to ease ahead at the end of a race, it isn't because he has run faster. It's because the other runners have slowed down. A sprinter should also run through the finish line. A good rule is to see the race as five yards further than it really is. Do not leap at the tape or celebrate too soon. A runner might lean forward from the waist the last step before the tape. If he leans too

Sprinters awaiting the gun must think about just one thing—running the race. Each runner should concentrate on himself and not worry about the person in the next lane. Here, you will notice that two of the runners have their right legs in the back block, while the other has his left leg back. Either way is correct.

In a running event, every split second can mean the difference between winning and losing. All runners must know the proper way to run the curves of an oval track. In general, the runner should stay as close to the inside of the track as he can. He should then lean his body slightly into the curve and pump his outside arm in the direction of the curve. By doing this in a relaxed way, he will lose very little speed while running the curve.

soon, he could blow it. So finish the way that feels most comfortable. Don't force a lean or a leap.

There was a time when the 220 yard or 200 meter dash was run in three parts. It started with the burst out of the blocks to full speed. Then the middle of the race was run relaxed, with perhaps just the slightest slackening of speed. Finally, there was a strong finishing burst in the final 40 to 50 yards. This is still a good way for young sprinters to run this race.

Most 200s are run around a curve or turn. The times in running the turn are slightly slower than those for a full straightaway. But it is very important to know how to run the turn. The two basic rules are to run as close as possible to the inside of the lane. This way, a runner is covering the shortest distance. The second rule is to lean inward because the speed of the body will tend to push it to the outside.

Learning How To Run A Relay

There is one other part of sprinting that all good runners will have to learn: running a relay, which combines speed and teamwork. There are some middle-distance relay races that aren't as difficult. In the shorter relays, in which each sprinter is running just 110 yards or 100 meters, teamwork is often the key to winning.

Relay runners must carry a baton while they're running. Then they must pass the baton to the next runner just as he is starting. The baton is a very light, hollow metal tube about a foot long.

The lead runner starts from the blocks, as always. The only difference is that he is holding the baton with his four fingers. He uses his thumb and knuckles for support as he leans into the blocks. The start and stride remain the same. So does the arm pumping technique, even though the runner has the baton.

The hard part and key to winning is the pass. This is the ex-

The blind baton pass is one of the keys to sprint relay success. The two runners here are about to execute the downward pass. They must practice together so that the lead runner can get a good running start when receiving the baton. The baton must be exchanged within a 20 meter (22-yard) passing zone. The lead runner here has extended his hand, palm up, and the trailing runner is about to make the pass with a downward motion.

change of the baton from one runner to another. If the pass is done right, a relay team does not lose a step. But if the pass does not go well, time and maybe the race will be lost. Should the baton be dropped during a pass, a team can kiss the race goodbye right then and there.

In a sprint relay, the sprinters use a pass called the *blind exchange*. That means the runner taking the pass does not look back at the incoming runner with the baton. He simply reaches back at the right moment and the incoming runner hands him the baton. Since both runners must be moving when the pass takes place, the blind exchange takes a great deal of practice.

During a relay race, there is a passing zone of about 22 yards. The pass must be made within this zone. If the baton is passed out of the zone, the team is disqualified. The outgoing runner can stand some 11 yards before the passing zone. This enables him to get a running start as the incoming runner prepares for the pass.

The outgoing runner sometimes makes one or two marks on the track before the passing zone. Some people call these "lean and go" marks. When the incoming runner reaches the first mark, the outgoing runner leans forward, ready to begin his sprint. At the second mark, the incoming runner will shout, "Go!" and the outgoing runner begins to sprint.

The pass should be made with runners extending their arms fully. It should take place no further than the middle of the passing zone. Then, if the baton is fumbled, there will be some room to recover. The pass should also be made with both runners going at nearly full speed.

There are two ways to take the baton. One is the *palm up* method. The outgoing runner reaches back with his palm up, and the incoming runner places the baton into his hand with a downward motion.

The *palm down* method is just the opposite. The outgoing runner reaches back with his palm down, and the incoming runner places the baton into his hand with an upward motion. In either case, just before the pass is made, the incoming runner should shout, "Now!" or "Hands!" or any other signal the teammates have decided on. Then, the outgoing runner can concentrate on his speed and the track but will know just when to expect the baton in his hand.

Most teams use an alternating-hand system of passes. That means that the lead runner will carry the baton in his right hand and pass it to the left hand of the second runner. The second person will carry it in his left hand and pass to the right hand of the

A successful pass is always made with a sure, firm motion. Passes in the sprint relays are always made to the opposite hand. The lead runner is taking the baton in his right hand from the left hand of the trailing runner. He will not switch hands during his leg of the race and will then pass the baton from his right hand into the left hand of the next runner. The incoming runner will often shout commands to the runner getting ready to take the pass. That also helps their timing on the exchange.

third runner. That runner will pass, in turn, to the left hand of the final runner. This method seems to produce smoother exchanges.

A few more tips. The outgoing runner should always keep the baton in the same hand with which he receives it. Trying to switch hands could slow him down or even cause the baton to drop. While running, he should hold the baton near the end, so he is ready to pass it to the next runner. This way, he won't have to make any adjustments close to the passing lane.

Incoming runners must also be careful after they've made the pass. They must stay in their lane until the other runners have passed, or they are sure the next lane is clear. An incoming runner who veers right or left after making a pass could crash into another sprinter. This is a good way to get hurt or have a team disqualified.

In the longer relays, the blind exchange is not necessary. The outgoing runner can turn and watch his teammate coming in. When the incoming man is close enough, the outgoing man begins running and extends his hand straight back to receive the baton. If the incoming man has the baton in his right hand, the outgoing runner should extend his left hand. Always use the opposite hand to receive the pass.

The outgoing runner in the distance relays may also switch hands once he has the stick, if he feels more comfortable that way. Because he isn't sprinting at full speed, there is less chance of a bobble when changing hands.

Running the relays can be fun. There is a real sense of team-work between teammates. If they all make perfect passes and win the race, they know they have really done something special.

Learning How To Run Middle And Long Distances

There have been many great middle and long distance runners. They may not have been fast enough to run sprints, but they had the stamina and heart to run farther. As a rule, the longer the race, the less the runner has to depend on speed. For young competitors, both the 400 and 800 meter races (or 440 and 880 yard runs) are middle distance. Starting with the 1,500 meter or mile, races become long distance. (By the way, a mile contains approximately 1,609 meters.)

There are two basic types of training methods that should be used by all middle and long distance runners. One is called *interval training*. Interval training is running a series of fairly short distances at a fast pace, with a short rest period in between. By doing this, the runner is purposely creating what is called an oxygen debt. Each time he runs and recovers, he improves slightly his body's ability to use oxygen well. Soon, his stamina will begin to improve. He can do this by running a number of 220 yard dashes, for example, at a fast pace.

While interval training is one way to improve stamina, *slow long-distance running* is another. By running very long distances at slow speeds, the runner is creating another healthy training tool. He is increasing the number of small blood vessels in his body. These are called capillaries, and they help the oxygen exchange process because they carry oxygen to the muscles.

As distances increase, the stride of a runner is shortened. The middle distance runner's stride is shorter than the sprinter's, but somewhat longer than the long distance runner's. The distance runners also do not use the same kind of high kick as the sprinters, and they are more erect when they run. While the sprinter runs totally on the soles of his feet, the middle distance runner uses the whole foot, from heel to toe.

Every runner has to find his own comfortable style. Any race with a number of runners will reveal a number of different styles and strides. A runner must find a comfortable stride that will allow him to run a relaxed pace. The more relaxed a runner, the less likely his muscles will tighten up.

There are some basic strategies for both the 400 and 800 meter middle distance runs. Both races are run around an oval track. Therefore, the method described earlier for running the turns in the 200 meter applies. The runner should lean into the turn and pump his opposite arm across his body.

Runners in the 400 should burst out of the blocks as if they were running a sprint. They should then continue to build up speed through the first turn. Then, when they come to the

Distance runners will shorten their strides and carry their arms lower. The pumping action is still rhythmic, but not as hard. The runner also uses heel-to-toe action with each stride. Middle and long-distance runners must also be relaxed and comfortable with their strides, conserving energy while maintaining a steady pace. The best distance runners seem to glide around the track in an effortless motion.

straightaway it is time for the relaxed stride. But the runner must try to stay as close to his top speed as he can.

Then comes the final turn. This is where the runners are getting tired, so it's important for them to drive around the turn while trying not to slow down. If the runner can keep a steady pace around the turn, he'll feel as if he is gaining speed off the turn.

It is important to stay relaxed in the final drive to the tape, because this is where the tired runner can really tighten up. He should run right through the tape and try to stay as relaxed as possible. The 400 isn't an easy race. More and more runners are looking at it as if it were a sprint. Therefore, a 400 runner must train hard and be ready to go all out.

With the 800, more racing strategy begins to come into play. Some runners like to set a fast pace, while others prefer to run behind the leaders. They would rather wait for a chance to make their move. Runners have to decide on the kind of strategy that is best for them.

For example, an 800 runner who doesn't have a lot of speed may want to run out front. By setting a fast pace, he may be able to tire out the runners behind him. This way, faster runners won't be able to outkick him at the finish. Sometimes front runners vary their speed. By speeding up, then slowing down, they can often confuse the runners behind them. These same strategies are used in even longer races.

By contrast, a runner with a lot of speed may just try to stay close to the leaders. He feels that his speed will win for him in the final straightaway. Runners must judge when the pace is too fast or too slow for their styles. They must also know when to make their moves. Because 800 meter runners do not go full speed for the entire race, they are able to sprint or kick at the end of the race.

Moving up to the 1,500, runners shorten their strides even more. There is also more heel to toe action than in the shorter races. But training is similar to that for the 800. The runner will have to build up his stamina for the longer distance. Interval training as well as slow long-distance running will be a part of all training programs. Distance runners also do speed work so they will be able to turn it on at the end.

Like all other runners, long-distance runners must be relaxed and comfortable. Their arm action should be normal and their breathing controlled. They do not have to pump nearly as hard as the sprinters, unless it is during their final kick. Distance runners, from the 800 on up, begin from a standing start. It's still good to get a fast start, especially in a large field. This way, a runner can get the position he or she wants without being boxed in.

The lead runners will always cut to the inside of the track with the other runners behind them. Passing should always be done on the outside. Inside, there just isn't enough room. In most

Racing strategy is all-important in distance running. A runner attempting to pass must always swing to the outside. She must do it either on a straightaway or coming off a curve. The passing runner must make a strong and decisive move to try to keep the other runner or runners from trying to pass her in turn. A runner trying to pass on the inside can often get boxed in, bumped, kicked or even spiked. So the passing runner must pick the spot, move to the outside and go!

cases, a runner will get himself in position on the outside shoulder of the runner in front of him. He will then try to pass with a sudden burst of speed.

It's best to pass on a straightaway or coming off a turn. Even better is to take the other runner by surprise. Pass quickly and try to open up a little distance right away. Otherwise, the other runner may try to pass in turn. Some runners also try to speed up to prevent being passed. Distance running can become a real cat-and-mouse game. Each runner tries to break the spirit of the other. Once a runner feels he cannot win the race, he's finished. Therefore, a distance runner must be strong of mind as well as strong of body.

42

Learning To Be A Hurdler

Hurdling has been described as sprinting over obstacles. It's far from easy to be sprinting at top speed and have to leap over a series of hurdles at the same time. Great hurdlers make it look easy, but they have practiced long and hard to reach their goal. All of them have taken their share of falls along the way.

A hurdler has to combine all the ingredients of sprinting with grace and timing because it is necessary to clear the hurdles without breaking stride or losing much time. In a sprint, the runners have to worry about their starts. Then it's a matter of reaching the tape as fast as they can. But with the hurdler, every step is important. One step out of stride and a hurdler can lose valuable time, and all the speed in the world won't matter.

Hurdling takes a great deal of practice to master. The hurdler must have speed and good timing, while also being aggressive. There are several ways to begin preparing for this difficult event. The hurdler should do all the warm-up exercises described earlier. Shown here is step one of an exercise to loosen up the muscles on the inside of the thigh, the ones used for hurdling. The hurdler is bending one leg back and resting it on the top of the hurdle.

In the Olympics, there are two hurdle races, the 110-meter high hurdles and the 400-meter intermediate hurdles. In the longer race, the hurdles aren't as high. Most high schools run three different hurdle races: the 110-meter highs, the 165-meter lows and the 300-meter intermediate hurdles. Each one takes a different technique.

The low hurdles are 30-inches high (but not run by girls); intermediate hurdles are 36-inches high (30 inches for girls); high hurdles are 39 inches off the ground (33 inches for girls). All hurdles are L shaped. The bottom of the L faces the hurdler, so if he hits the hurdle it will tip away from him. A hurdler can continue in a race if he hits one or all the hurdles. However, hitting the hurdles will throw his timing off and slow him down.

Hurdlers must work on their techniques. To begin with, they don't jump over the hurdles, even though it might look that way. A hurdler really steps over the hurdle one leg at a time. His lead leg will be the same leg he uses to kick that football or soccer ball, and it will be his back leg in the starting blocks. In the shorter,

After the hurdler rests her leg on the top of the hurdle, she then bends down and touches the ground in front of her other leg, which is held straight. This should be done slowly and held for five or ten seconds. If there is pain or discomfort, she should stop. The exercise is done with each leg taking a turn on the hurdle.

high hurdle race, the lead leg never changes. In the longer races, some hurdlers will lead with either leg, depending on their strides.

One good way for a beginning hurdler to get a feel for the sport is to set up a low hurdle. The point is to practice jumping alongside the hurdle, not over it. Then he should run just to the side of it with his lead leg, planting his foot about 10 to 12 inches beyond the hurdle. As he does this, he will lean forward and bring his trailing leg over the hurdle. The trailing leg should come down in front of the lead foot.

The beginner should continue doing this to see how natural it feels to bring that trailing leg over the hurdle. The natural hurdler is going to feel comfortable with this movement very quickly. The drill can be done with three or four hurdles in a row. Next, the

This is an excellent drill to enable the new hurdler to get used to the actual motion of the jump. It is done by setting up a low hurdle, then running just to the side of it with the lead leg. But the trailing leg should be lifted over the hurdle, sweeping over the bar and landing in front of the lead foot. As a rule, the lead foot should be planted about 10 to 12 inches in front of the hurdle as the back leg sweeps over. The more the hurdler does this, the more he should try to snap the back leg over in a hard, quick motion. This is what he will have to do once he begins to race.

When approaching the hurdle, the runner begins her jump by leaning forward as she lifts her lead leg and pushes off with her trailing leg.

As the front leg clears the hurdle. The opposite arm is thrust forward for balance and momentum. The hurdler must now get ready to bring the trailing leg over. She must still lean forward and turn the toe of the rear foot outward to make sure it doesn't hit the crossbar.

46

At the midway point of the leap, the hurdler is still leaning forward ready to snap the trailing leg through the jump. If the hurdler begins to straighten up too soon, there is more of a chance of the trailing leg catching the hurdle.

The trailing leg over, the hurdler now begins to come straight down with the lead leg. At this point, a good hurdler is ready to resume sprinting and is thinking about her steps to the next barrier. She should come straight over the hurdle, with shoulders parallel to the finish line.

The hurdler lands with the lead leg, then immediately drives forward with the trailing leg to regain the sprinting motion between hurdles. An experienced hurdler will know exactly how many steps to take between each hurdle and must concentrate on form and speed throughout the race.

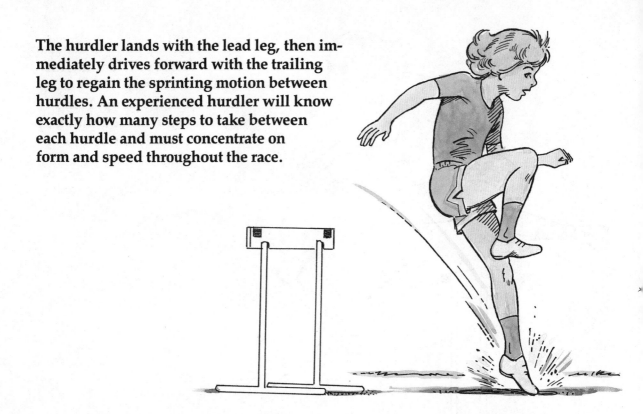

drill is done by leaping with the lead foot as it passes alongside the hurdle. Again, the hurdler brings the trailing foot over.

Finally it's time for some actual hurdling. The approach should be straight ahead at about half speed. The hurdler should try to time it right and stretch the lead leg straight over the hurdle. The trailing leg should follow the same way it did in the drills. It is important to lean forward. When the thigh of the hurdler's trailing leg is parallel to the crossbar, he should pull the leg over hard, almost snapping it down. It is this quick step and snap that will get him quickly over each hurdle.

Each step takes the young hurdler closer to an actual race. Soon he will be going over three or four hurdles, placing them racing distance apart. He will get a sense of the number of steps he must take between hurdles. This depends on his stride, which he may have to adjust.

The more hurdles he takes, the more his confidence will grow. Soon, he will be almost attacking the hurdles, going hard over them and landing without breaking stride. Now he is well on his way to becoming a competitive hurdler.

But there is still more. Now it's time to go out and run an actual course. For young runners, it's best to begin with low hurdles. Once he or she is comfortable about running the low hurdles, it's time to try the intermediate and finally the highs. The basic hurdling technique is the same for all three. Only the distances are different.

For instance, most hurdlers will take off about 6½ to 7 feet before the hurdle. The takeoff point should be the same each time. That's why the stride and number of steps is so important. Most hurdlers will take seven or eight strides from the start to the first high hurdle. In the low hurdles, they will take 10 strides to the first jump; in the intermediates, about 21 to 23 strides before the first hurdle.

Each hurdler must work out what is best for him or her and stick with it. In the high hurdles, there are just three strides between hurdles. In the lows, there are usually seven strides in between, and in the intermediates, 15 to 17 strides. This is why hurdlers are always working on their "steps." If a stride is broken or the steps are just not right, the hurdler just cannot run a smooth race.

There are 10 hurdles to clear in a high hurdles race, and eight each in the lows and intermediates. With the short distance between hurdles, precise technique is most important in a high hurdles race. In the longer races, the hurdler can make some adjustments during the race, but they can only be minor ones and not too many. Every second still counts.

While the hurdles are made to tip when hit, every hurdler takes a fall now and then. This is something the hurdler cannot worry about. Once he begins to think about falling, his times will suffer because he will no longer be attacking the hurdles.

If a runner is always hitting the hurdles with the ankle of his

Between hurdles, the hurdler resumes the high-knee, arm-pumping technique of a sprinter. There is a shorter distance between the high hurdles than there is between the low and intermediate hurdles. While the hurdling technique is basically the same, the technique between hurdles in the different events may change slightly.

trailing leg, he should try leaning forward more as he takes off. The lean should be from the waist. If this does not correct the problem, then he may be snapping his trailing leg through too soon. He should try waiting a split second longer before bringing the trailing leg through the hurdle.

By the same token, if the lead leg is hitting the hurdle, then it's probably a problem in the takeoff. The hurdler may be taking off too close to the hurdle. Correcting this is just a matter of adjusting stride. Also, when a runner is going over a hurdle, the arm opposite his lead leg should come forward. This creates the best hurdling balance.

It takes a long time to become a good hurdler. The hurdles are not events a young competitor should try unless he really wants to do it. A good coach can see which team members will make the best hurdlers. He will be able to teach the technique, as well as mapping out a good training program for new hurdlers to follow.

Learning The High Jump And Long Jump

The high jump and the long jump are both similar and different. Both are field events in which the competitors must jump for height and distance. The high jump relies on strength, leaping ability and very good technique. The long jump (formerly called the broad jump) relies a good deal on speed and athletic ability.

While high jump techniques have changed quite a bit over the years, the long jump has remained basically the same. At first glance, it may seem that both events are relatively easy. One is designed to see how high someone can jump, and the other to see how far. As with other track and field events, to become very good takes hours of practice, hard training and a good coach.

The first rule of thumb for a high jumper is to learn to jump upward, not forward. A young jumper might think that because he has to run toward the bar he must leap forward over it, but a jumper who leaps forward will not be able to get the height needed for success.

Years ago, high jumpers used a scissors kick. They would be almost upright going over the bar and land on their feet. Soon after, jumpers began using different kinds of roll techniques. They would approach the bar from an angle, kick the front leg up, then roll their body over the bar before scissoring the back leg over.

With the roll, the high jumper would clear the bar face down. He would then flip over and land on his back. Using the roll technique, high jumpers went over the seven-foot mark for the first time. Before long, there was another new style of jumping, and it is still used by most high jumpers today.

It was originally called the Fosbury Flop, though today it is generally referred to as simply the flop. Dick Fosbury, who was on the 1968 Olympic team, was the first high jumper to go over the bar backwards. Some laughed when they first saw the Fos-

Today, almost all high jumpers use the Fosbury Flop or plain flop technique. They begin by approaching the bar at about a 35 degree angle. A high jumper must judge his steps so that his takeoff step will be with his outside leg.

bury Flop. But when Dick Fosbury won the Olympic Gold Medal with a leap of 7'4½", the laughing stopped.

Chances are that almost all young jumpers starting out today will be taught the flop style by their coaches. However, jumpers must be sure they are jumping into a large and very soft pit area. High jumpers using the flop technique will be landing on the upper back and neck, so they need a soft pit to avoid injuries.

The flop also gives the jumper a chance to better use the speed he builds up during his approach run. This approach should be at an angle of 35 degrees to the bar. Unlike the other styles of

The jumper must work to get tremendous thrust from his outside leg. He will also lift the knee of his inside leg to help propel him into the jump. As he takes off, he will begin to turn his body so that his back is to the bar.

jumping, a flop jumper uses his outside foot for the initial push upward. Other styles used the inside foot. If a flop jumper approaches the bar from the left side, he will jump off his right foot.

Most jumpers use an approach of 7 to 11 strides, depending on what approach distance is most comfortable. Like hurdlers, high jumpers must measure their steps so they will end up in a perfect position for their take off. Using the flop, it's important for the jumper not to turn his back on the bar too soon.

Before making that turn, the jumper should drive his left knee and right arm upward. He does this just as he pushes off the

53

As he clears the bar, his back is completely turned. When his hips have cleared the bar, he must straighten his knees and raise his legs so that they will also fall over the bar and not hit it on the way down.

right foot. As he drives upward, the jumper should turn his left or inside shoulder away from the bar. This begins the movement to turn his entire back to the bar. By the time the shoulder is higher than the bar, the jumper's back should be facing the bar.

At that point, the jumper should tip his head back and begin to arch his hips above the crossbar. Once the hips have gone over the bar, he must quickly raise his knees and forelegs so they, too, will clear the bar. Since raising the knees and legs forces the hips downwards, the jumper must wait until the hips are clear of the

A high jumper using the flop style will land on his neck, shoulder and back. So he must be sure to jump into a pit that is well-padded with soft foam or he may injure himself. Like most jumping events, high jumping requires a good coach and many hours of practice.

bar before raising his knees. He will then come straight down backwards, landing on his back and neck.

While all of these points are important to a successful jump, it's extremely important for the jumper to get that initial upward thrust. He must learn to use his speed, then drive hard with his left knee and right arm. He must also push very hard off his outside foot, generating more of the power that will propel him over the bar.

To do all this well, the high jumper should have a great deal of power in his legs and arms. Once again, the coach can provide a series of exercises designed to improve high jump performance.

The long jump is a combination of speed, timing and jumping ability. Long jumpers will run from 100 to 150 feet down a straight runway before taking off on their jump. Every good jumper knows that to jump far, he must jump high. To do this, he has to explode off the mark for the height needed to get real distance.

A long jumper begins to build his power during his approach run. It is really like a sprint. The jumper must be relaxed, taking long strides with high knee action. He has to maintain top speed right to the point of takeoff. Jumpers usually mark a checkpoint somewhere before the takeoff board that tells them how close they are getting to their jump.

The takeoff is very important. Because the jumper will hit the take off board at top speed, he must be able to judge his steps without breaking stride. The jumper needs to get tremendous thrust and push with his take off leg. To help do this, he will lower his hips just before the takeoff. He must also kick hard with his lead leg, bringing his knee up high to help him get the height he will need.

Some jumpers prefer to just soar through the air, chin and chest up, back slightly arched. They trail their feet a little behind. The jumper here is using another method. It sometimes looks as if the jumper is still running when he is in the air. He is actually kicking his legs in an effort to get more distance.

The final stride to the board is a slightly shorter stride. This allows momentum to bring the body forward and helps create more power for the takeoff. The head must be kept up as well. The jumper should not look at the board, making steps and timing so important.

The heel of the takeoff foot hits the board first. The jumper will flex his knee for just a second and then straighten it as his body rocks forward onto the ball of the foot. This movement must be practiced again and again. It is the beginning of the jump, and it must create an explosive upward action.

As the jumper nears his landing point, he swings his hips and legs forward, almost straightening his knees. He also throws his arms forward to help his balance and to help keep him from falling backwards.

If the jumper is going off his left foot, he will drive both his right knee and left arm upward. When he leaves the board, his hips and upper body should be moving ahead of the takeoff foot. The knee of the takeoff leg then drives forward and upward.

Once in the air, the jumper rotates his right arm in a circular motion. He also rotates the left leg (the takeoff leg), then extends both legs in front of him for the landing. The heels should make contact with the pit first. At contact, the jumper will throw his head and shoulders forward and downward. He will then fall forward and wind up on his hands and knees. The jump will be measured from the end of the takeoff board to the first heel mark in the pit.

The above jump is often called the *step-in-air style*. Some jumpers prefer the *hang style*. In the hang style, the jumper glides through the air with the legs down and slightly behind him. Just before landing, he swings his arms and feet forward for extra

As soon as he touches the pit, the jumper bends at the knees and leans forward, dropping his head forward as well. The jump will be measured from the end of the takeoff board to the first mark from the landing in the sand.

length. It takes strong abdominal muscles to make this final movement.)

Like all other track and field athletes, long jumpers must be in top shape. They must warm up and stretch before each workout. A pulled muscle can be a nagging, long-term injury. It's best to try to avoid them. Stretching is the best way.

Strength helps all track and field athletes. A good coach will know just which muscle groups have to be strengthened for each event. Then he can map out a series of exercises. Some track and field competitors now work with weights and strength machines. This, too, should only be done on the advice of a coach. The wrong exercises can be harmful.

Track and field is a popular and healthy sport for boys and girls. Those who start young can improve slowly and pick the events they like best. Track is for athletes of any age. It's never too late to get started in some forms of the sport and to do them well.

Track and field is a fun sport and a great conditioner for the body. But it is also highly competitive, a team sport as well as an individual one. It's really satisfying to beat your best time and know you are improving. But better yet is crossing the finish line first and feeling your chest breaking that tape while the crowd roars in the background.

Glossary

Approach   Term used to describe the run prior to the long jump and high jump events.

Back roll   A form of high jumping in which the jumper rolls over the bar face down, then lands on his back.

Bar   The cross support over which the high jumper must leap. If the bar is hit, it will fall off its side supports, giving the jumper a miss.

Baton   The lightweight, hollow metal tube about a foot long that relay runners must carry and then pass to their teammates.

Blind exchange or pass   A relay pass in which the runner receiving the pass does not look at the runner making it.

Flats   Name given to lightweight running shoes, used for training, and which contain no spikes.

Fosbury Flop   Style of high jumping named after Olympic champion Dick Fosbury. In the flop, the jumper goes over the bar backwards.

Gun   Refers to the starter's gun. The starter fires a pistol containing blank cartridges to begin each race.

Hamstring stretch   Important warm-up exercise in which the muscles in the back of a runner's legs are stretched. The runner puts one leg up on a rail or similar support and reaches for the outstretched foot with both hands.

Hang style   A form of long jumping in which the jumper glides through the air with his legs down and slightly behind him.

Hurdler's stretch   Another important warmup exercise done by sitting down and folding one leg to the rear, with the other outstretched in front. The athlete then reaches forward for the outstretched foot by bending forward at the waist.

Hurdling   Track events in which runners must jump barriers or hurdles of a specific height and set a specific distance apart.

Interval training   A training method in which the runner alternately sprints very hard, then jogs, repeating the process a number of times.

Long distance   Running events of 1,500 meters, a mile, or longer.

Middle distance   Running events of 400 and 800 meters, or 440 yards and the half mile.

Pass   The exchange of the baton between two runners.

Passing zone   An area in which the baton must be passed or else the relay team is disqualified.

Pit   A well-padded area in which the high jumper lands. Also, the sanded area in which the long jumper lands.

Relay A running event in which four runners comprise a team, each running one-quarter, or leg, of the total distance in the event.

Runway A 100 to 150 foot approach to the long jump that gives jumpers a chance to build up speed for the takeoff.

Scissors kick Another method of high jumping in which jumpers go over the bar nearly upright and land on their feet.

Speed work Name given to various training methods used to increase a sprinter's speed.

Split stretch Another warmup exercise done with feet spread wide apart, legs straight. The athlete bends at the waist and touches the right hand to the left toe, then the left hand to the right toe, standing straight up in between.

Sprints Short events run at full speed, such as the 100 and 200 meter dashes, or the 100 and 220 yard dashes.

Stamina The strength to run longer distances at faster speed without getting tired. A good runner will train to build up stamina and cut his time.

Starting blocks Special adjustable supports that anchor in the track and allow sprinters to push off for the fastest times possible.

Step in air Another style of long jumping in which the jumper seems to take an additional running step as he soars through the air.

Steps Term used to describe a high jumper or long jumper's final approach before takeoff. The jumper must get the timing of his steps just right to achieve the best takeoff. The term also refers to the correct number of strides between hurdles.

Takeoff board A wooden board used as the takeoff point for the long jump. If any part of the runner's foot goes over the front of the board on takeoff, the jump is illegal.